ABRAHAM'S VOICES

ABRAHAM'S VOICES

Lorraine Healy

World Enough Writers

ISBN 978-1-937797-02-7

Cover and interior photos by Lorraine Healy

Author photo by Dianne MoonDancer

Book and Cover Design by Tonya Namura
using Liberation Serif

World Enough Writers
c/o Lana Ayers
PO Box 1808
Kingston, WA 98346

http://worldenoughwriters.com
WorldEnoughWriters@gmail.com

For Alicia Suskin Ostriker

Table of Contents

ABRAHAM'S VOICES

sarai, close to Egypt

he said—and there were stars
heard him—
you are beyond lovely

and I fear for my
life—how can the powerful
abstain from you?

let us say this:

let us, he said,
us
and it was night
and the moon heard it

his god allowed this

abraham

who stretches on the cooling
ground filled with unyielding
and stares at the night's edges

until a wild gallop courses him
up and down
and he is

convinced
aroused like a young goat
such the certainty

and the women look from a distance
as he talks himself empty
into the silent air

they decide who
will open a dry, tired crotch
to appease the old kook

and let the encampment sleep—
the others whose eyes pity
wife and slave, joint jugs

plunked into the dusty well,
the exhausted shepherds
whose seed is exactly like his own

but only Abraham flaps
relentless beyond the mound
of animals at rest, who walks

pulling the thread of voices
he alone senses in the air
and the women fear this story

he is weaving out of frayed
gusts of hardened wind

hagar

what I wanted was homeland
not old man

she had first-born ways
but also sweetness

and filled the road to the well
with tales of Ur and her laughter

what I wanted was water-drenched—
if not freedom, a more merciful sun

the illusion of sister, peaceful tents—
to be made of cool air

but their god gave me her furious
regret after his tenderness, his scant seed—

here is my treasure of son, here
a solitude wide as a god's promise

ishmael

He shall be a wild ass of a man,
his hand against every man
Gen. 17.12

the prophecies of night sky
speak of my father

the man who could read and inscribe
                turned God's nomad

twice Sarah, the shriveled one,
banished us to the places of thirst

twice she allowed my father
to stop by the land of my hunting

but forbade him to dismount—
astride his camel, beholding my absence

they were invisible, his blessing
and his scent, yet I returned

and smelled him—old age and animal and distance—
I am of his herd forever

lot's wife

I looked ahead   only ahead
as we left the weeping terah
for months of dusty road all I looked at
was lot's tawny neck
the back of abram's head

I dropped daughters every place
we dwelled   Harran
and Egypt   Mamre   Sodom
I walked and suckled child
and looked around me

there was already sulphur
in the air and dead sparrows
on the ground on the trail
to Zoar   what was I
leaving behind   what
my two grown girls
and their houses
and their babes

what else was I leaving
my name

isaac

I have been fooled
repeatedly

my meekness   a garment soiled

three days I rode behind my father's
stony face, brimful with questions

upon returning I had no voice
for moons and moons

when it came back,
it would forever stall on the tent flaps

of my mouth,   every word
needing to suspend in air

waiting for its angel

*

my father bound me
                              a tie
of yes to his voices
a rope smelling
of animal
                    and my terror

upon returning
                    my mother
a small package
of tight white bandage

what remains
of her laughter   smeared
over my name

*

under his knife I was
his woman   his slave
his beast
of burden   one endless yes
to the voices in his head

*

and when the words
came back
                    to my tongue
seasons had changed

it was too late
my lips too used
                    to binds

the voice I had left
a hapless spurt
a thing at which
                    to laugh

the ram

a silent leopard would have taken me
or a wolf as solitary as myself—
the old man was swift
and not unkind, set me on the cairn
with my head facing east
so the morning star would find me
      his young one   to the side
      he was a pile of small rocks
      was a crumbled altar   its stones rolling downhill

lord of the Steepest, sure-hoofed One,
i used to lie on bedding of pebbles and scant grasses,
rest one horn on the ground
through the darkness
my foreleg extended
and the horn would dream

the old man took my horns and where
they dangled on the small
of his back   the mountain wind
skewered a sound
out of them— a sorrowful bleat
that blows deep into the twilight,
the sound of ewes coming upon
a slope of hacked new lambs

sarah

by the time I wake there are roads
of silence every direction
by the time I set bread
on the coals of night
they are gone   gone

what have you done with my
laughter, old man?
                        wind dry as a tent wall
hits everything I see

something has taken a turn
for the worse, the careless heel
of God's hand has skewed the horizon line
overnight   I am
tilting
                        has a messenger come
to say who is dying, who is to blame
for the broken honey jars
                                    give me
someone to punish
someone to cast out
                        to be thirsty
and alone and lit with madness
because every road rushes downwards
every sound is the bruise of thunder
every wind howls from behind

keturah

he was ancient
but still
made me some babes

and he'd hold them
in those crumbling stone hands
rock them through colic
and night
babbling sweetly
about Ur
about the road

that god of his
stayed silent
even as the man
folded
back and back
onto his death

not a word
from the unnameable

I thought to myself   some
god

the land speaks

at the loss end of his life
he paid four hundred shekels
for a cave—
an emptiness   on the side
of a wall of white rock

paid a man who had come
from the same far-off place
he had, whose claim

on me was lesser
than an ant's   hours they took,
a herd of preening men
bartering dust

abram ben terah knew a thing
or two about possession
never claimed gods' promises
brought his coin purse

the place he bought
would be his house of bones
already a room for his linen-wrapped
beloved

how many times his god told him
I was his, his, his
from water to water?
his to pass on
and on
along his line of stars?

gods can be as deluded
as any creature in heat

but abram knew

the only currency that claims a deed
on me
is dead flesh on dead bone

when what was you
looks no different than powdered shale,
than lime,
that's when the land
is yours

Notes

On the poems

sarai, close to Egypt: Gen.12:10

hagar: Gen.16:7-14 and 21:9-21

ishmael: Gen.16:7-14 and 21:9-21, as well as some of the Ibrahim/Abraham stories that come from the Islamic tradition.

lot's wife: Gen.19:17-26

isaac: Gen.22:1-20

the ram: Gen.22:13-14. The references to the ram being potential prey to a leopard or lone wolves come from *Fauna and Flora of the Bible. Help for Translators,* volume XI. London, United Bible Societies, 1972. pp 48 and 85.

sarah: Gen.22:1-20 and 23:1-2

keturah: Gen.25:1-4

On the artwork

All of the artwork is a combination of my own digital and film photographs, with the exception of the Hebrew parchment underlying the photograph of Abraham, Sarah, and Hagar on the cover (it's a copy of the earliest extant form of Hebrew script, which I found on the Internet). The photographs of Sumerian artifacts were taken at the Musée du Louvre, Paris, and the ones of religious statuary at the Chartres and Rouen Cathedrals, France, in January 2012. For reasons of printing and costs, the artwork in this chapbook was converted to B&W. For the original color images, please visit my web site: www. Lorrainehealy.com

Acknowledgements

My gratitude to Alicia S. Ostriker, mentor and poet extraordinaire, for opening this path for me and for her prodding and advice; to Sharon "Shoe" Shoemaker, for unstinting, unceasing support, friendship, mentorship, and good humor; to Hedgebrook, where some of these poems were written during one of two wonderful residencies; to Evie Lindstrom Wilson, magician librarian, for the wealth of information and arcana she discovered on Abraham; to Lana Hechtman Ayers, Jim Bertolino, and Brent Allard of World Enough Writers, for their faith in "Abraham's Voices."

Bows of thanks also to Diane "Diva" Divelbess, Janlori Goldman, Diana Deering, the Poetry Pod, Randall Mullins and Sharon Pavelda, all first readers of these poems. Diva Divelbess' informal lecture on the historical/archeological background to the mythical Abraham's journey from Sumer to Harran to Canaan was absolutely invaluable in freeing my imagination to what I could find in the interstices of the biblical text. Tons of gratitude to theologian Wes Howard-Brook of Seattle University for reading the poems and providing the back cover blurb.

To Dianne and Phoebe MoonDancer: *thanks* doesn't even begin to cover it. Besos to you both.

About the Author

Lorraine Healy is an award-winning Argentinean poet who has been published extensively. Nominated for a Pushcart in 2004, she has a M.F.A from the New England College and a post-MFA from Antioch University Los Angeles. She is the first poet to have received a green card solely on the merits of her work. A winner of the Patricia Libby First Book Award, her book *The Habit of Buenos Aires* was selected by David St. John and published by Tebot Bach in 2010. She has just completed her second full-length book, currently looking for a press. A Hedgebrook alumna and a fine-arts photographer, Lorraine has long made her home on Whidbey Island, Washington.

www.ingramcontent.com/pod-product-compliance
Lightning Source LLC
Chambersburg PA
CBHW032110040426
42449CB00007B/1236